CONGESTIVE HEART FAILURE COOKBOOK FOR NEWLY DIAGNOSED

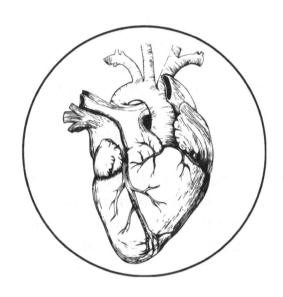

NO SALT RECIPES FOR HEALTHY HEART

TABLE OF CONTENTS

INTRODUCTION

If you're holding this cookbook, you've likely been diagnosed with congestive heart failure (CHF). That can be a lot to take in, and it's completely normal to feel overwhelmed. But take a deep breath—you're not alone, and there are many ways to manage this condition and still enjoy delicious meals.

Understanding Congestive Heart Failure

Congestive heart failure is a condition where the heart doesn't pump blood as efficiently as it should. This inefficiency can lead to a buildup of fluids in the body, causing symptoms like shortness of breath, fatigue, and swelling in the legs and ankles. It sounds serious because it is, but with the right lifestyle changes, including a heart-healthy diet, you can improve your quality of life.

Why No Salt?

One of the key dietary adjustments for managing CHF is reducing sodium intake. Sodium causes your body to retain water, increasing the burden on your heart. Cutting down on salt can help reduce fluid buildup and ease the workload on your heart. This might sound daunting, especially if you're used to seasoning your food liberally. But don't worry, you don't have to sacrifice flavor for health.

This cookbook is your guide to navigating a new, no-salt culinary world. It's filled with recipes that are both heart-friendly and satisfying. You'll find that with the right ingredients and techniques, you can create meals that are bursting with flavor, all without a grain of salt. These recipes will help you maintain a healthier lifestyle while still enjoying the foods you love.

CHAPTER 1

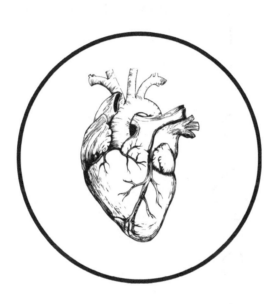

BREAKFAST RECIPES

Oatmeal with Fresh Berries and Almonds

INGREDIENTS

- 1 cup rolled oats
- 2 cups water or unsweetened almond milk
- 1/2 cup fresh berries (strawberries, blueberries, raspberries)
- 2 tbsp sliced almonds
- 1 tbsp honey (optional)
- 1/2 tsp cinnamon (optional)

Preparation Time:
- 5 minutes

Cooking Time:
- 10 minutes

DIRECTIONS

1. In a medium saucepan, bring water or almond milk to a boil.
2. Add oats and turn the heat down to low. Cook for 5-7 minutes, stirring occasionally, until oats are tender.
3. Top with fresh berries, sliced almonds, honey, and cinnamon if desired.

NUTRITIONAL INFORMATION

- Calories: 300
- Protein: 10g
- Fat: 10g
- Carbs: 45g
- Sodium: 10mg

Greek Yogurt with Sliced Strawberries and Chia Seeds

INGREDIENTS

- 1 cup plain Greek yogurt
- 1/2 cup sliced strawberries
- 1 tbsp chia seeds
- 1 tbsp honey (optional)

DIRECTIONS

1. Spoon Greek yogurt into a bowl.
2. Top with sliced strawberries and chia seeds.
3. Drizzle with honey if desired.

NUTRITIONAL INFORMATION

- Calories: 200
- Protein: 15g
- Fat: 5g
- Carbs: 25g
- Sodium: 70mg

Preparation Time:
- 5 minutes

Cooking Time:
- None

SPINACH AND MUSHROOM EGG WHITE OMELETTE

INGREDIENTS

- 4 egg whites
- 1/2 cup fresh spinach, chopped
- 1/2 cup mushrooms, sliced
- 1 tbsp olive oil
- 1/4 tsp black pepper
- 1/4 tsp garlic powder

DIRECTIONS

1. Heat olive oil in a non-stick skillet over medium heat.
2. Add mushrooms and cook until soft, about 3-4 minutes.
3. Add spinach and cook until wilted, about 1-2 minutes.
4. In a bowl, whisk egg whites with black pepper and garlic powder.
5. Pour egg whites into the skillet and cook until set, about 3-4 minutes. Fold and serve.

NUTRITIONAL INFORMATION

- Calories: 150
- Protein: 20g
- Fat: 7g
- Carbs: 5g
- Sodium: 150mg

Preparation Time:
- 5 minutes

Cooking Time:
- 10 minutes

Avocado and Tomato on Whole Grain Toast

INGREDIENTS

- 1 ripe avocado
- 1 medium tomato, sliced
- 2 slices whole grain bread
- 1/4 tsp black pepper
- 1/4 tsp garlic powder
- 1/2 lemon, juiced

DIRECTIONS

1. Toast the whole grain bread slices.
2. Mash the avocado in a bowl with black pepper, garlic powder, and lemon juice.
3. Spread mashed avocado on toast.
4. Top with sliced tomato.

Preparation Time:
- 5 minutes

Cooking Time:
- 2 minutes (toasting bread)

NUTRITIONAL INFORMATION

- Calories: 300
- Protein: 7g
- Fat: 20g
- Carbs: 30g
- Sodium: 120mg

Fruit Smoothie with Kale and Flaxseed

INGREDIENTS

- 1 cup kale leaves, stems removed
- 1 banana
- 1/2 cup frozen mixed berries
- 1 tbsp flaxseed meal
- 1 cup unsweetened almond milk
- 1/2 cup water

DIRECTIONS

1. Combine all ingredients in a blender.
2. Blend until smooth.
3. Pour into a glass and drink right away.

Preparation Time:
- 5 minutes

Cooking Time:
- None

NUTRITIONAL INFORMATION

- Calories: 200
- Protein: 4g
- Fat: 5g
- Carbs: 35g
- Sodium: 40mg

Quinoa Porridge with Apples and Cinnamon

INGREDIENTS

- 1 cup quinoa
- 2 cups water
- 1 apple, chopped
- 1/2 tsp ground cinnamon
- 1 tbsp honey (optional)
- 1/4 cup unsweetened almond milk

DIRECTIONS

1. Rinse quinoa under cold water.
2. Boil water in a medium pot. Add quinoa, lower the heat, and cook for 15 minutes until the quinoa is soft and the water is gone.
3. Stir in chopped apple, ground cinnamon, and honey if using.
4. Serve with a splash of almond milk.

Preparation Time:
- 5 minutes

Cooking Time:
- 20 minutes

NUTRITIONAL INFORMATION

- Calories: 250
- Protein: 6g
- Fat: 4g
- Carbs: 48g
- Sodium: 10mg

COTTAGE CHEESE WITH PINEAPPLE AND WALNUTS

INGREDIENTS

- 1 cup low-fat cottage cheese
- 1/2 cup fresh pineapple chunks
- 2 tbsp chopped walnuts

DIRECTIONS

1. Spoon cottage cheese into a bowl.
2. Top with fresh pineapple chunks and chopped walnuts.

Preparation Time:
- 5 minutes

Cooking Time:
- None

NUTRITIONAL INFORMATION

- Calories: 200
- Protein: 18g
- Fat: 8g
- Carbs: 16g
- Sodium: 400mg

Banana Pancakes with Blueberries

INGREDIENTS

- 1 ripe banana
- 2 large eggs
- 1/2 cup fresh blueberries
- 1/4 tsp ground cinnamon
- 1 tsp olive oil

DIRECTIONS

1. In a bowl, mash the banana. Add eggs and cinnamon, and mix well.
2. Heat olive oil in a non-stick skillet over medium temperature.
3. Pour batter into the skillet to form small pancakes. Cook for 2-3 minutes on each side, until it becomes golden brown.
4. Top with fresh blueberries.

Preparation Time:
- 5 minutes

Cooking Time:
- 10 minutes

NUTRITIONAL INFORMATION

- Calories: 250
- Protein: 10g
- Fat: 10g
- Carbs: 32g
- Sodium: 70mg

SWEET POTATO AND BLACK BEAN BREAKFAST BURRITO

INGREDIENTS

- 1 medium sweet potato, peeled and diced
- 1/2 cup black beans, rinsed and drained
- 2 large eggs
- 1 tbsp olive oil
- 1/4 tsp black pepper
- 1 whole grain tortilla

DIRECTIONS

1. Heat olive oil in a skillet over medium temperature. Add sweet potato and cook until tender, about 10 minutes.
2. Add black beans and cook until heated through, about 2 minutes.
3. In a different pan, scramble the eggs.
4. Combine sweet potato mixture and scrambled eggs in the tortilla. Season with black pepper and roll up to form a burrito.

Preparation Time:
- 10 minutes

Cooking Time:
- 15 minutes

NUTRITIONAL INFORMATION

- Calories: 350
- Protein: 15g
- Fat: 14g
- Carbs: 45g
- Sodium: 150mg

Homemade Muesli with Almond Milk and Fresh Fruits

INGREDIENTS

- 1 cup rolled oats
- 1/4 cup chopped nuts
(almonds, walnuts)
- 1/4 cup raisins or
dricd cranberries
- 1/2 cup fresh fruit
(berries, banana slices,
apple chunks)
- 1 cup unsweetened
almond milk

DIRECTIONS

1. In a bowl, combine rolled oats, chopped nuts, and dried fruit.
2. Serve with fresh fruit and almond milk.

Preparation Time:
- 5 minutes

Cooking Time:
- None

NUTRITIONAL INFORMATION

- Calories: 300
- Protein: 7g
- Fat: 10g
- Carbs: 45g
- Sodium: 10mg

CHAPTER 2

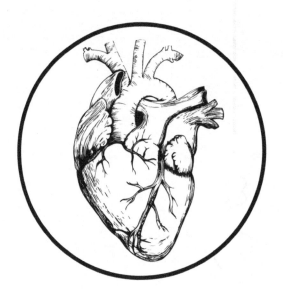

LUNCH RECIPES

GRILLED CHICKEN SALAD WITH AVOCADO AND LIME DRESSING

INGREDIENTS

- 2 boneless, and skinless chicken breasts
- 1 avocado, diced
- 4 cups mixed greens
- 1 cup cherry tomatoes, halved
- 1/4 cup red onion, thinly sliced
- 1/4 cup olive oil
- 2 tbsp lime juice
- 1/4 tsp black pepper
- 1/4 tsp garlic powder

DIRECTIONS

1. Preheat grill to medium-high heat. Season chicken breasts with black pepper and garlic powder.
2. Grill chicken for 5-7 minutes on each side, until cooked through. Let stay for five minutes, then slice.
3. In a large bowl, combine mixed greens, cherry tomatoes, red onion, and avocado.
4. In a small bowl, whisk together olive oil and lime juice.
5. Drizzle dressing over salad and top with grilled chicken.

Preparation Time:
- 10 minutes

Cooking Time:
- 15 minutes

NUTRITIONAL INFORMATION

- Calories: 400
- Protein: 30g
- Fat: 25g
- Carbs: 12g
- Sodium: 75mg

QUINOA AND BLACK BEAN STUFFED BELL PEPPERS

INGREDIENTS

- 4 bell peppers, tops cut off and seeds removed
- 1 cup quinoa
- 1 1/2 cups water
- 1 can (15 oz) black beans, rinsed and drained
- 1 cup corn kernels (fresh or frozen)
- 1 cup diced tomatoes
- 1/4 cup chopped cilantro
- 1/2 tsp cumin
- 1/2 tsp black pepper

Preparation Time:
- 15 minutes

Cooking Time:
- 40 minutes

DIRECTIONS

1. Preheat oven to 375°F (190°C).
2. Rinse quinoa and combine with water in a medium saucepan. Bring to a boil, then reduce heat and simmer for 15 minutes until water is absorbed and quinoa is tender.
3. In a large bowl, mix cooked quinoa, black beans, corn, diced tomatoes, cilantro, cumin, and black pepper.
4. Stuff bell peppers with the quinoa mixture and place in a baking dish.
5. Cover with foil and bake for 30 minutes. Then, take off the foil and bake for 10 more minutes.

NUTRITIONAL INFORMATION

- Calories: 250
- Protein: 8g
- Fat: 4g
- Carbs: 48g
- Sodium: 10mg

BAKED SALMON WITH ASPARAGUS AND LEMON

INGREDIENTS

- 2 salmon fillets (4 oz each)
- 1 bunch asparagus, trimmed
- 1 lemon, thinly sliced
- 2 tbsp olive oil
- 1/4 tsp black pepper
- 1/4 tsp garlic powder

DIRECTIONS

1. Preheat oven to 400°F (200°C).
2. Put the salmon fillets and asparagus on a baking sheet. Drizzle with olive oil and sprinkle with black pepper and garlic powder.
3. Arrange lemon slices over salmon and asparagus.
4. Bake for 15-20 minutes, until salmon is cooked through and asparagus is tender.

Preparation Time:
- 10 minutes

Cooking Time:
- 20 minutes

NUTRITIONAL INFORMATION

- Calories: 350
- Protein: 25g
- Fat: 25g
- Carbs: 10g
- Sodium: 60mg

Turkey and Spinach Lettuce Wraps

INGREDIENTS

- 1 lb ground turkey
- 1 cup fresh spinach, chopped
- 1/4 cup finely diced onion
- 2 cloves garlic, minced
- 1 tbsp olive oil
- 1/4 tsp black pepper
- 1/4 tsp paprika
- Large lettuce leaves (e.g., romaine or butter lettuce) for wrapping

DIRECTIONS

1. Heat olive oil in a skillet over medium temperature. Add onion and garlic, and cook until soft.
2. Add ground turkey, black pepper, and paprika. Cook until turkey it becomes browned and cooked through.
3. Stir in chopped spinach and cook until wilted.
4. Serve turkey mixture in large lettuce leaves.

Preparation Time:
- 10 minutes

Cooking Time:
- 15 minutes

NUTRITIONAL INFORMATION

- Calories: 250
- Protein: 30g
- Fat: 12g
- Carbs: 4g
- Sodium: 80mg

VEGETABLE STIR-FRY WITH TOFU

INGREDIENTS

- 1 block (14 oz) firm tofu, drained and cubed
- 1 cup broccoli florets
- 1 cup sliced bell peppers
- 1 cup snap peas
- 1/2 cup sliced carrots
- 2 tbsp olive oil
- 1/4 cup low-sodium soy sauce (or tamari for gluten-free)
- 2 cloves garlic, minced
- 1 tsp grated ginger
- 1/4 tsp black pepper

DIRECTIONS

1. Heat 1 tbsp olive oil in a large skillet or wok over medium-high heat. Put tofu and cook until it is golden brown on all sides. Remove and set aside.
2. Add remaining olive oil to the skillet. Put garlic and ginger, and cook it for one minute.
3. Add broccoli, bell peppers, snap peas, and carrots. Stir-fry for 5 to 7 minutes until vegetables become tender-crisp.
4. Return tofu to the skillet. Add low-sodium soy sauce and black pepper, and stir to combine.

Preparation Time:
- 10 minutes

Cooking Time:
- 15 minutes

NUTRITIONAL INFORMATION

- Calories: 250
- Protein: 15g
- Fat: 14g
- Carbs: 18g
- Sodium: 150mg

LENTIL SOUP WITH CARROTS AND CELERY

INGREDIENTS

- 1 cup dried lentils, rinsed
- 4 cups low-sodium vegetable broth
- 2 carrots, diced
- 2 celery stalks, diced
- 1 onion, diced
- 2 cloves garlic, minced
- 1 tbsp olive oil
- 1/2 tsp black pepper
- 1/2 tsp dried thyme
- 1/2 tsp dried oregano

DIRECTIONS

1. Heat olive oil in a big pot over medium temperature. Put onion and garlic, and cook until it becomes soften.
2. Add carrots and celery, and cook for 5 minutes.
3. Stir in lentils, vegetable broth, black pepper, thyme, and oregano.
4. Bring to a boil, then reduce heat and simmer for 30-40 minutes, until lentils and vegetables are tender.

Preparation Time:
- 10 minutes

Cooking Time:
- 40 minutes

NUTRITIONAL INFORMATION

- Calories: 250
- Protein: 15g
- Fat: 6g
- Carbs: 40g
- Sodium: 50mg

CHICKPEA AND TOMATO SALAD WITH OLIVE OIL AND BASIL

INGREDIENTS

- 1 can (15 oz) chickpeas, rinsed and drained
- 1 cup cherry tomatoes, halved
- 1/4 cup red onion, finely diced
- 2 tbsp olive oil
- 1 tbsp balsamic vinegar
- 1/4 cup fresh basil leaves, chopped
- 1/4 tsp black pepper

DIRECTIONS

1. In a large bowl, combine chickpeas, cherry tomatoes, red onion, and basil.
2. In a small bowl, whisk together olive oil, balsamic vinegar, and black pepper.
3. Pour the dressing over salad and toss to combine well.

Preparation Time:
- 10 minutes

Cooking Time:
- None

NUTRITIONAL INFORMATION

- Calories: 220
- Protein: 7g
- Fat: 12g
- Carbs: 24g
- Sodium: 30mg

Zucchini Noodles with Pesto and Cherry Tomatoes

INGREDIENTS

- 2 medium zucchinis, spiralized
- 1 cup cherry tomatoes, halved
- 1/4 cup homemade pesto (basil, olive oil, garlic, pine nuts, no salt)
- 1 tbsp olive oil
- 1/4 tsp black pepper

DIRECTIONS

1. Heat olive oil in a big skillet over medium temperature.
2. Add zucchini noodles and cherry tomatoes. Cook for 3-4 minutes until zucchini is just tender.
3. Remove from heat and toss with pesto and black pepper.

Preparation Time:
- 10 minutes

Cooking Time:
- 5 minutes

NUTRITIONAL INFORMATION

- Calories: 180
- Protein: 4g
- Fat: 16g
- Carbs: 10g
- Sodium: 25mg

CHICKEN AND VEGETABLE SKEWERS

INGREDIENTS

- 2 boneless, and skinless chicken breasts, cut into cubes
- 1 red bell pepper, cut into chunks
- 1 yellow bell pepper, cut into chunks
- 1 zucchini, sliced
- 1 red onion, cut into chunks
- 2 tbsp olive oil
- 1 tbsp lemon juice
- 1/2 tsp black pepper
- 1/2 tsp dried oregano

DIRECTIONS

1. Preheat grill to medium-high temperature.
2. In a bowl, combine olive oil, lemon juice, black pepper, and oregano.
3. Thread chicken and vegetables onto skewers.
4. Brush with olive oil mixture.
5. Grill skewers for 10-12 minutes, turning occasionally, until chicken is cooked through.

Preparation Time:
- 15 minutes

Cooking Time:
- 12 minutes

NUTRITIONAL INFORMATION

- Calories: 300
- Protein: 25g
- Fat: 15g
- Carbs: 12g
- Sodium: 70mg

Eggplant and Tomato Bake with Fresh Herbs

INGREDIENTS

- 1 large eggplant, sliced
- 2 cups cherry tomatoes, halved
- 2 tbsp olive oil
- 1/4 cup fresh basil leaves, chopped
- 1/4 cup fresh parsley, chopped
- 2 cloves garlic, minced
- 1/4 tsp black pepper

DIRECTIONS

1. Preheat oven to 375°F (190°C).
2. Place eggplant slices on a baking sheet. Drizzle with 1 tbsp olive oil and roast for 20 minutes.
3. In a bowl, combine cherry tomatoes, remaining olive oil, garlic, black pepper, basil, and parsley.
4. Remove eggplant from oven and top with tomato mixture.
5. Return to oven and bake for an additional 15 minutes.

Preparation Time:
- 10 minutes

Cooking Time:
- 35 minutes

NUTRITIONAL INFORMATION

- Calories: 200
- Protein: 3g
- Fat: 14g
- Carbs: 18g
- Sodium: 20mg

CHAPTER 3

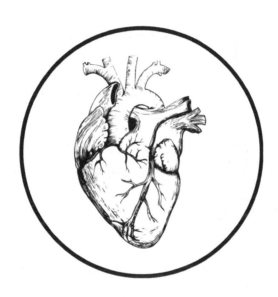

DINNER RECIPES

GRILLED LEMON HERB CHICKEN WITH ROASTED VEGETABLES

INGREDIENTS

- 2 boneless, skinless chicken breasts
- 1 lemon, juiced
- 2 tbsp olive oil
- 2 cloves garlic, minced
- 1 tsp dried thyme
- 1 tsp dried rosemary
- 1 tsp dried oregano
- 2 cups of mixed vegetables (bell peppers, zucchini, carrots), chopped
- Cooking spray

Preparation Time:
- 40 minutes

Cooking Time:
- 20 minutes

DIRECTIONS

1. In a bowl, mix lemon juice, olive oil, garlic, thyme, rosemary, and oregano all together.
2. Marinate chicken breasts in the mixture for 30 minutes.
3. Preheat grill to medium-high heat. Grill chicken for 6-8 minutes per side, until cooked through.
4. Meanwhile, toss mixed vegetables with a little olive oil and spread them on a baking sheet.
5. Roast vegetables in the oven at 400°F (200°C) for 20-25 minutes, until it is tender.
6. Serve grilled chicken with roasted vegetables.

NUTRITIONAL INFORMATION

- Calories: 250
- Protein: 30g
- Fat: 12g
- Carbs: 10g
- Sodium: 50mg

Baked Cod with Garlic and Herbs

INGREDIENTS

- 2 cod fillets
- 2 cloves garlic, minced
- 2 tbsp olive oil
- 1 tsp dried parsley
- 1 tsp dried thyme
- 1/2 tsp black pepper
- Lemon wedges for serving

DIRECTIONS

1. Preheat oven to 400°F (200°C).
2. Place cod fillets on a baking dish covered with parchment paper.
3. In a small bowl, mix together minced garlic, olive oil, parsley, thyme, and black pepper.
4. Spread the garlic herb mixture evenly over the cod fillets.
5. Bake for 12-15 minutes, until the fish is opaque and flakes easily with a fork.
6. Serve with lemon wedges.

Preparation Time:
- 10 minutes

Cooking Time:
- 15 minutes

NUTRITIONAL INFORMATION

- Calories: 200
- Protein: 25g
- Fat: 10g
- Carbs: 2g
- Sodium: 40mg

SPAGHETTI SQUASH WITH TOMATO BASIL SAUCE

INGREDIENTS

- 1 spaghetti squash
- 2 cups tomato basil sauce (homemade or store-bought)
- Fresh basil leaves for garnish

DIRECTIONS

1. Preheat oven to 400°F (200°C).
2. Cut spaghetti squash into two equal half and remove the seeds.
3. Place squash halves cut side down on a baking sheet covered with parchment paper.
4. Bake for 40-45 minutes, until squash becomes tender.
5. Let squash cool slightly, then use a fork to scrape the flesh into spaghetti-like strands.
6. Heat tomato basil sauce in a saucepan over medium temperature.
7. Serve spaghetti squash topped with tomato basil sauce. Garnish with fresh basil leaves.

Preparation Time:
- 10 minutes

Cooking Time:
- 45 minutes

NUTRITIONAL INFORMATION

- Calories: 100
- Protein: 2g
- Fat: 2g
- Carbs: 20g
- Sodium: 20mg

TURKEY MEATLOAF WITH MASHED CAULIFLOWER

INGREDIENTS

- 1 lb ground turkey
- 1/2 cup breadcrumbs (made from whole grain bread)
- 1/4 cup milk (dairy or non-dairy)
- 1 egg
- 1/4 cup finely diced onion
- 2 cloves garlic, minced
- 1 tsp dried thyme
- 1 tsp dried rosemary
- 1/2 tsp black pepper
- 1 large cauliflower, cut into florets
- 2 tbsp olive oil
- Fresh parsley for garnish

Preparation Time:
- 20 minutes

Cooking Time:
- 45 minutes

DIRECTIONS

1. Preheat oven to 375°F (190°C).
2. In a big bowl, mix ground turkey, breadcrumbs, milk, egg, onion, garlic, thyme, rosemary, and black pepper all together.
3. Transfer the turkey mixture to a loaf pan and shape into a loaf.
4. Bake for 40-45 minutes, until cooked through.
5. Meanwhile, steam cauliflower florets until tender.
6. Transfer steamed cauliflower to a food processor and add olive oil. Blend until smooth and creamy.
7. Serve slices of turkey meatloaf with mashed cauliflower. Garnish with fresh parsley.

NUTRITIONAL INFORMATION

- Calories: 300
- Protein: 25g
- Fat: 15g
- Carbs: 15g
- Sodium: 60mg

STIR-FRIED TOFU WITH BROCCOLI AND BELL PEPPERS

INGREDIENTS

- 1 block (14 oz) firm tofu, drained and cubed
- 2 cups broccoli florets
- 1 red bell pepper, sliced
- 1 yellow bell pepper, sliced
- 2 cloves garlic, minced
- 2 tbsp olive oil
- 1/4 cup low-sodium soy sauce (or tamari for gluten-free)
- 1 tsp grated ginger
- 1/2 tsp black pepper

DIRECTIONS

1. Heat olive oil in a large skillet or wok over medium-high temperature.
2. Put minced garlic and grated ginger. Cook for 1 minute.
3. Put tofu cubes and cook until golden brown on all sides. Bring the tofu from the skillet and set put aside.
4. In the same skillet, add broccoli florets and bell pepper slices. Stir-fry for 5-7 minutes until vegetables become tender-crisp.
5. Return tofu to the skillet. Pour in low-sodium soy sauce and sprinkle with black pepper.
6. Stir-fry for another 2-3 minutes until everything is heated through.
7. Serve hot, garnished with sesame seeds if desired.

Preparation Time:
- 15 minutes

Cooking Time:
- 15 minutes

NUTRITIONAL INFORMATION

- Calories: 250
- Protein: 15g
- Fat: 15g
- Carbs: 15g
- Sodium: 60mg

ROASTED VEGETABLE QUINOA BOWL

INGREDIENTS

- 1 cup quinoa
- 2 cups water
- 2 cups of mixed vegetables (bell peppers, zucchini, carrots), chopped
- 2 tbsp olive oil
- 1 tsp dried thyme
- 1 tsp dried rosemary
- 1/2 tsp black pepper

DIRECTIONS

1. Wash the quinoa with cold water. Then, in a pot, boil some water. Add the quinoa and lower the heat. Let it cook for 15 minutes until it's soft and the water is gone.

2. Preheat oven to 400°F (200°C). Put the mixed vegetables on a baking sheet covered with parchment paper. Add olive oil, dried thyme, dried rosemary, and black pepper. Cook in the oven for 20-25 minutes until the vegetables are soft.

3. In a bowl, layer cooked quinoa and roasted vegetables.

4. Serve hot as a nutritious and satisfying meal.

NUTRITIONAL INFORMATION

- Calories: 300
- Protein: 8g
- Fat: 10g
- Carbs: 45g
- Sodium: 20mg

Preparation Time:
- 10 minutes

Cooking Time:
- 25 minutes

-

Lemon Garlic Shrimp with Steamed Asparagus

INGREDIENTS

- 1 lb big shrimp, peeled and deveined
- 2 cloves garlic, minced
- 1 lemon, juiced and zested
- 2 tbsp olive oil
- 1/4 tsp black pepper
- 1 bunch asparagus, trimmed

DIRECTIONS

1. In a bowl, toss shrimp with minced garlic, lemon juice, lemon zest, olive oil, and black pepper. Let marinate for 15 minutes.
2. Heat a large skillet over medium-high temperature. Add shrimp and cook for 2-3 minutes per side until it turns pink and cooked through.
3. While the shrimp is cooking, steam asparagus until tender-crisp, about 3-4 minutes.
4. Serve shrimp with steamed asparagus.

Preparation Time:
- 10 minutes

Cooking Time:
- 10 minutes

NUTRITIONAL INFORMATION
- Calories: 200
- Protein: 25g
- Fat: 10g
- Carbs: 5g
- Sodium: 20mg

OVEN-ROASTED CHICKEN THIGHS WITH BRUSSELS SPROUTS

INGREDIENTS

- 4 chicken thighs, bone-in and skin-on
- 2 cups Brussels sprouts, trimmed and halved
- 2 tbsp olive oil
- 2 cloves garlic, minced
- 1 lemon, juiced
- 1 tsp dried thyme
- 1/2 tsp black pepper

DIRECTIONS

1. Preheat oven to 400°F (200°C).
2. In a bowl, mix olive oil, minced garlic, lemon juice, dried thyme, and black pepper all together.
3. Put the chicken thighs and Brussels sprouts on a baking sheet covered with parchment paper.
4. Pour olive oil mixture over chicken and Brussels sprouts, making sure they are evenly coated.
5. Roast in the oven for 25 to 30 minutes, until chicken becomes golden brown and cooked through.
6. Serve hot as a delicious and nutritious meal.

NUTRITIONAL INFORMATION

- Calories: 300
- Protein: 25g
- Fat: 15g
- Carbs: 10g
- Sodium: 30mg

Preparation Time:
- 10 minutes

Cooking Time:
- 30 minutes

EGGPLANT AND ZUCCHINI RATATOUILLE

INGREDIENTS

- 1 eggplant, diced
- 2 zucchinis, diced
- 1 bell pepper, diced
- 1 onion, diced
- 2 cloves garlic, minced
- 2 tbsp olive oil
- 1 can (14 oz) diced tomatoes
- 1 tsp dried basil
- 1 tsp dried oregano
- 1/2 tsp black pepper

DIRECTIONS

1. Heat olive oil in a large skillet over medium temperature. Put diced onion and garlic, and cook until it softens.
2. Put diced eggplant, zucchini, bell pepper, diced tomatoes, basil, oregano, and black pepper to the skillet.
3. Cover and simmer for 20 to 25 minutes, stirring occasionally, until vegetables become tender.
4. Serve hot as a main dish or side.

Preparation Time:
- 10 minutes

Cooking Time:
- 25 minutes

NUTRITIONAL INFORMATION

- Calories: 150
- Protein: 3g
- Fat: 7g
- Carbs: 20g
- Sodium: 20mg

LENTIL AND VEGETABLE CURRY

INGREDIENTS

- 1 cup dried lentils, rinsed
- 2 cups low-sodium vegetable broth
- 1 onion, diced
- 2 cloves garlic, minced
- 1 bell pepper, diced
- 1 zucchini, diced
- 1 carrot, diced
- 1 can (14 oz) coconut milk
- 2 tbsp curry powder
- 1 tsp ground turmeric
- 1/2 tsp black pepper
- Fresh cilantro for garnish

Preparation Time:
- 10 minutes

Cooking Time:
- 30 minutes

DIRECTIONS

1. In a big pot, combine lentils, vegetable broth, diced onion, minced garlic, diced bell pepper, diced zucchini, and diced carrot.
2. Bring to a boil, then lower the heat and simmer for 20 to 25 minutes, until lentils become tender.
3. Stir in coconut milk, curry powder, turmeric, and black pepper. Simmer for another 5 to10 minutes.
4. Serve hot, garnished with fresh cilantro.

NUTRITIONAL INFORMATION

- Calories: 250
- Protein: 10g
- Fat: 10g
- Carbs: 30g
- Sodium: 50mg

CHAPTER 4

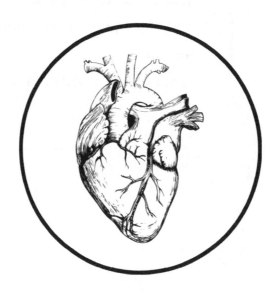

SMOOTHIES

BERRY BLAST SMOOTHIE

INGREDIENTS

- 1 cup mixed berries (which includes strawberries, blueberries, raspberries)
- 1 banana, sliced
- 1/2 cup plain Greek yogurt
- 1/2 cup almond milk
- 1 tbsp honey (optional)

DIRECTIONS

1. Combine all ingredients in a blender.
2. Blend until it is smooth.
3. Serve immediately.

NUTRITIONAL INFORMATION

- Calories: 200
- Protein: 8g
- Fat: 3g
- Carbohydrates: 35g
- Fiber: 6g
- Sugar: 22g
- Sodium: 50mg

GREEN GODDESS SMOOTHIE

INGREDIENTS

- 1 cup spinach leaves
- 1/2 cup cucumber, diced
- 1/2 avocado, peeled and pitted
- 1/2 banana, sliced
- 1/2 cup coconut water

DIRECTIONS

1. Place all ingredients in a blender.
2. Blend until it is smooth.
3. Pour into a glass and enjoy!

NUTRITIONAL INFORMATION

- Calories: 180
- Protein: 4g
- Fat: 11g
- Carbohydrates: 20g
- Fiber: 8g
- Sugar: 7g
- Sodium: 80mg

TROPICAL PARADISE SMOOTHIE

INGREDIENTS

- 1/2 cup pineapple chunks
- 1/2 cup mango chunks
- 1/2 banana, sliced
- 1/2 cup coconut milk
- 1/4 cup orange juice

DIRECTIONS

1. Combine all ingredients in a blender.
2. Blend until it is smooth and creamy.
3. Pour into a glass and serve chilled.

NUTRITIONAL INFORMATION

- Calories: 250
- Protein: 3g
- Fat: 9g
- Carbohydrates: 40g
- Fiber: 4g
- Sugar: 28g
- Sodium: 20mg

Citrus Sunrise Smoothie

INGREDIENTS

- 1 orange, peeled and segmented
- 1/2 cup strawberries, hulled
- 1/2 banana, sliced
- 1/2 cup Greek yogurt
- 1/4 cup almond milk

DIRECTIONS

1. Put all ingredients in a blender.
2. Blend until it is smooth.
3. Pour into a glass and enjoy the refreshing taste of citrus.

NUTRITIONAL INFORMATION

- Calories: 180
- Protein: 8g
- Fat: 2g
- Carbohydrates: 35g
- Fiber: 6g
- Sugar: 22g
- Sodium: 40mg

CREAMY AVOCADO SMOOTHIE

INGREDIENTS

- 1/2 ripe avocado, peeled and pitted
- 1/2 cup spinach leaves
- 1/2 banana, sliced
- 1/2 cup almond milk
- 1 tbsp honey (optional)

DIRECTIONS

1. Combine all ingredients in a blender.
2. Blend until it is smooth and creamy.
3. Pour into a glass and serve it immediately.

NUTRITIONAL INFORMATION

- Calories: 220
- Protein: 4g
- Fat: 12g
- Carbohydrates: 26g
- Fiber: 6g
- Sugar: 16g
- Sodium: 50mg

BEETROOT BERRY SMOOTHIE

INGREDIENTS

- 1 small beetroot, cooked and peeled
- 1/2 cup of mixed berries (which includes strawberries, blueberries, raspberries)
- 1/2 banana, sliced
- 1/2 cup Greek yogurt
- 1/2 cup almond milk
- 1 tbsp honey (optional)

DIRECTIONS

1. Put all ingredients in a blender.
2. Blend until it is smooth and creamy.
3. Pour into a glass and serve chilled.

NUTRITIONAL INFORMATION

- Calories: 180
- Protein: 8g
- Fat: 2g
- Carbohydrates: 35g
- Fiber: 7g
- Sugar: 25g
- Sodium: 40mg

PINEAPPLE SPINACH SMOOTHIE

INGREDIENTS

- 1 cup fresh pineapple chunks
- 1 cup spinach leaves
- 1/2 banana, sliced
- 1/2 cup coconut water
- Juice of 1/2 lime
- 1 tbsp honey (optional)

DIRECTIONS

1. Combine all ingredients in a blender.
2. Blend until it is smooth and creamy.
3. Pour into a glass and enjoy the tropical goodness.

NUTRITIONAL INFORMATION

- Calories: 160
- Protein: 3g
- Fat: 1g
- Carbohydrates: 38g
- Fiber: 5g
- Sugar: 25g
- Sodium: 30mg

Mango Banana Smoothie

INGREDIENTS

- 1 cup mango chunks
- 1/2 banana, sliced
- 1/2 cup Greek yogurt
- 1/2 cup almond milk
- 1 tbsp honey (optional)
- Dash of ground cinnamon (optional)

DIRECTIONS

1. Put all ingredients into a blender.
2. Blend until it is smooth and creamy.
3. Pour into a glass and garnish with a sprinkle of ground cinnamon if desired.

NUTRITIONAL INFORMATION

- Calories: 210
- Protein: 8g
- Fat: 3g
- Carbohydrates: 40g
- Fiber: 4g
- Sugar: 32g
- Sodium: 50mg

BLUEBERRY KALE SMOOTHIE

INGREDIENTS

- 1/2 cup blueberries
- 1 cup kale leaves, stemmed
- 1/2 banana, sliced
- 1/2 cup Greek yogurt
- 1/2 cup almond milk
- 1 tbsp honey (optional)

DIRECTIONS

1. Combine all ingredients in a blender.
2. Blend until it is smooth and creamy.
3. Pour into a glass and enjoy the nutritious boost of blueberries and kale.

NUTRITIONAL INFORMATION

- Calories: 200
- Protein: 7g
- Fat: 3g
- Carbohydrates: 38g
- Fiber: 6g
- Sugar: 25g
- Sodium: 50mg

PEACH ALMOND SMOOTHIE

INGREDIENTS

- 1 cup frozen peach slices
- 1/2 banana, sliced
- 1/4 cup almonds
- 1/2 cup Greek yogurt
- 1/2 cup almond milk
- 1 tbsp honey (optional)

DIRECTIONS

1. Put all ingredients into a blender.
2. Blend until it is smooth and creamy.
3. Pour into a glass and enjoy the delightful combination of peaches and almonds.

NUTRITIONAL INFORMATION

- Calories: 250
- Protein: 9g
- Fat: 9g
- Carbohydrates: 35g
- Fiber: 6g
- Sugar: 26g
- Sodium: 50mg

Chapter 5

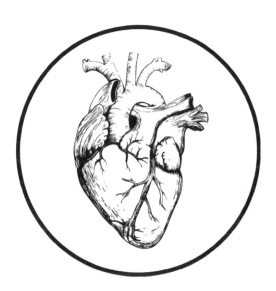

Dessert

MIXED BERRY PARFAIT

INGREDIENTS

- 1 cup of mixed berries (like strawberries, blueberries, raspberries)
- 1 cup Greek yogurt
- 1/4 cup granola
- 1 tbsp honey (optional)

DIRECTIONS

1. In a glass or bowl, put mixed berries, Greek yogurt, and granola in layers.
2. Repeat the layers until the glass or bowl is full.
3. Drizzle honey on top if desired.
4. Serve immediately or refrigerate until ready to serve.

NUTRITIONAL INFORMATION

- Calories: 220
- Protein: 14g
- Fat: 3g
- Carbohydrates: 40g
- Fiber: 6g
- Sugar: 24g
- Sodium: 60mg

BANANA "NICE" CREAM

INGREDIENTS

- 2 ripe bananas, peeled and sliced
- 1/4 cup almond milk (or any milk of choice)
- 1 tsp vanilla extract
- Optional toppings: sliced strawberries, chopped nuts, shredded coconut

DIRECTIONS

1. Put sliced bananas in a single layer on a baking sheet covered with parchment paper.
2. Freeze it for at least 2 hours or until solid.
3. Transfer the frozen bananas to a blender or food processor.
4. Add almond milk and vanilla extract.
5. Blend until it is smooth and creamy, scraping down the sides as needed.
6. Serve immediately as soft-serve ice cream or freeze for a firmer texture.
7. Top with sliced strawberries, chopped nuts, or shredded coconut if desired.

NUTRITIONAL INFORMATION

- Calories: 150
- Protein: 2g
- Fat: 1g
- Carbohydrates: 35g
- Fiber: 4g
- Sugar: 18g
- Sodium: 5mg

BAKED APPLES WITH CINNAMON

INGREDIENTS

- 2 apples, cored and halved
- 1 tsp cinnamon
- 1 tbsp honey (optional)
- Optional toppings: chopped nuts, raisins, Greek yogurt

DIRECTIONS

1. Preheat the oven to 375°F (190°C).
2. Put apple halves in a baking dish.
3. Sprinkle cinnamon over the apples and drizzle with honey if desired.
4. Bake for 20-25 minutes or until the apples are tender.
5. Serve warm, topped with chopped nuts, raisins, or a dollop of Greek yogurt if desired.

NUTRITIONAL INFORMATION

- Calories: 100
- Protein: 1g
- Fat: 0g
- Carbohydrates: 27g
- Fiber: 5g
- Sugar: 20g
- Sodium: 0mg

DARK CHOCOLATE AVOCADO MOUSSE

INGREDIENTS

- 2 ripe avocados, peeled and pitted
- 1/4 cup unsweetened cocoa powder
- 1/4 cup honey or maple syrup
- 1 tsp vanilla extract
- Optional toppings: sliced strawberries, shaved dark chocolate

DIRECTIONS

1. Place avocados, cocoa powder, honey or maple syrup, and vanilla extract in a blender or food processor.
2. Blend until it is smooth and creamy, scraping down the sides as needed.
3. Transfer the mousse to serving bowls or glasses.
4. Refrigerate it for at least 30 minutes to chill.
5. Serve topped with sliced strawberries and shaved dark chocolate if desired.

NUTRITIONAL INFORMATION

- Calories: 180
- Protein: 2g
- Fat: 11g
- Carbohydrates: 22g
- Fiber: 6g
- Sugar: 13g
- Sodium: 5mg

PEACH SORBET

INGREDIENTS

- 2 cups frozen peach slices
- 1/4 cup honey or maple syrup
- 1 tbsp lemon juice
- Optional garnish: mint leaves

DIRECTIONS

1. Place frozen peach slices, honey or maple syrup, and lemon juice in a blender or food processor.
2. Blend until it is smooth and creamy.
3. Transfer the mixture to a shallow dish and freeze for 4-6 hours or until firm.
4. Use a fork to scrape the surface of the sorbet to create a fluffy texture.
5. Serve in bowls or glasses, garnished with mint leaves if desired.

NUTRITIONAL INFORMATION

- Calories: 120
- Protein: 1g
- Fat: 0g
- Carbohydrates: 31g
- Fiber: 3g
- Sugar: 28g
- Sodium: 0mg

BERRY CHIA SEED PUDDING

INGREDIENTS

- 1/4 cup chia seeds
- 1 cup of almond milk
(or any milk of choice)
- 1 tbsp honey or maple
syrup
- 1/2 cup of mixed
berries (like
strawberries,
blueberries,
raspberries)

DIRECTIONS

1. In a bowl, mix chia seeds, almond milk, and
honey or maple syrup.
2. Stir well and let it sit for 5 minutes.
3. Stir again to break up any clumps of chia seeds.
4. Cover and refrigerate it overnight or for at least
4 hours.
5. Before serving, layer the chia pudding and
mixed berries in glasses or bowls.
6. Serve chilled.

NUTRITIONAL INFORMATION

- Calories: 180
- Protein: 5g
- Fat: 8g
- Carbohydrates: 22g
- Fiber: 9g
- Sugar: 10g
- Sodium: 80mg

MANGO COCONUT POPSICLES

INGREDIENTS

- 2 ripe mangoes, peeled and diced
- 1/2 cup coconut milk
- 2 tbsp honey or maple syrup
- Optional: shredded coconut for garnish

DIRECTIONS

1. Place diced mangoes, coconut milk, and honey or maple syrup in a blender.
2. Blend until smooth.
3. Pour the mixture into popsicle molds.
4. Insert popsicle sticks into the molds.
5. Freeze for at least 4 hours or until firm.
6. Before serving, run warm water over the molds to loosen the popsicles.
7. Optionally, sprinkle shredded coconut over the popsicles before serving.

NUTRITIONAL INFORMATION

- Calories: 120
- Protein: 1g
- Fat: 4g
- Carbohydrates: 22g
- Fiber: 2g
- Sugar: 20g
- Sodium: 5mg

Strawberry Yogurt Bark

INGREDIENTS

- 1 cup Greek yogurt
- 1 cup sliced strawberries
- 2 tbsp honey or maple syrup
- Optional toppings: sliced almonds, shredded coconut

DIRECTIONS

1. Put parchment paper on a baking sheet.
2. Put Greek yogurt evenly on the parchment paper.
3. Arrange sliced strawberries on top of the yogurt.
4. Pour honey or maple syrup over the strawberries.
5. Optionally, sprinkle sliced almonds or shredded coconut over the top.
6. Freeze for 2-3 hours or until firm.
7. Break the yogurt bark into pieces before serving.

NUTRITIONAL INFORMATION

- Calories: 120
- Protein: 6g
- Fat: 3g
- Carbohydrates: 18g
- Fiber: 2g
- Sugar: 14g
- Sodium: 30mg

Lemon Blueberry Oat Bars

INGREDIENTS

- 1 cup rolled oats
- 1/2 cup almond flour
- 1/4 cup honey or maple syrup
- 1/4 cup coconut oil, melted
- Zest and juice of 1 lemon
- 1 cup blueberries

DIRECTIONS

1. Preheat the oven to 350°F (175°C). Grease a baking dish or line it with parchment paper.
2. In a big bowl, combine rolled oats, almond flour, honey or maple syrup, melted coconut oil, lemon zest, and lemon juice. Mix well.
3. Gently fold in the blueberries.
4. Press the mixture into the prepared baking dish, spreading it out evenly.
5. Bake for 20-25 minutes or until it is golden brown.
6. Allow to cool completely before slicing into bars.
7. Serve and enjoy!

NUTRITIONAL INFORMATION

- Calories: 180
- Protein: 3g
- Fat: 9g
- Carbohydrates: 24g
- Fiber: 3g
- Sugar: 12g
- Sodium: 0mg

GRILLED PINEAPPLE WITH HONEY DRIZZLE

INGREDIENTS

- 1 pineapple, peeled and cored, cut into rings or wedges
- 2 tbsp honey
- Optional: mint leaves for garnish

DIRECTIONS

1. Preheat the grill to medium temperature.
2. Grill the pineapple slices for 2-3 minutes on each side, until grill marks appear and pineapple is heated through.
3. Remove the pineapple from the grill and place on a serving platter.
4. Pour the honey over the grilled pineapple.
5. You can garnish it with mint leaves if you want.
6. Serve warm.

NUTRITIONAL INFORMATION

- Calories: 100
- Protein: 1g
- Fat: 0g
- Carbohydrates: 27g
- Fiber: 2g

CHAPTER 6

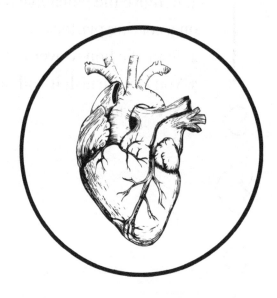

SNACKS

APPLE SLICES WITH ALMOND BUTTER

INGREDIENTS

- 1 apple, sliced
- 2 tbsp almond butter

DIRECTIONS

1. Wash and slice the apple.
2. Spread almond butter on the apple slices.

NUTRITIONAL INFORMATION

- Calories: 200
- Protein: 4g
- Fat: 14g
- Carbohydrates: 17g
- Fiber: 4g
- Sugar: 11g
- Sodium: 0mg

Carrot Sticks with Hummus

INGREDIENTS

- 2 carrots, cut into sticks
- 1/4 cup hummus

DIRECTIONS

1. Wash and cut carrots into sticks.
2. Serve with hummus for dipping.

NUTRITIONAL INFORMATION

- Calories: 120
- Protein: 3g
- Fat: 6g
- Carbohydrates: 14g
- Fiber: 5g
- Sugar: 4g
- Sodium: 0mg

Greek Yogurt with Sliced Peaches

INGREDIENTS

- 1/2 cup Greek yogurt
- 1 peach, sliced

DIRECTIONS

1. Place Greek yogurt in a bowl.
2. Top with sliced peaches.

NUTRITIONAL INFORMATION

- Calories: 150
- Protein: 12g
- Fat: 0g
- Carbohydrates: 22g
- Fiber: 2g
- Sugar: 18g
- Sodium: 0mg

RICE CAKES WITH AVOCADO MASH

INGREDIENTS

- 2 rice cakes
- 1 avocado, mashed

DIRECTIONS

1. Spread mashed avocado on rice cakes.

NUTRITIONAL INFORMATION

- Calories: 180
- Protein: 3g
- Fat: 10g
- Carbohydrates: 21g
- Fiber: 6g
- Sugar: 0g
- Sodium: 0mg

CELERY STICKS WITH PEANUT BUTTER

INGREDIENTS

- 4 celery sticks
- 2 tbsp peanut butter

DIRECTIONS

1. Wash and cut celery into sticks.
2. Spread peanut butter on celery sticks.

NUTRITIONAL INFORMATION

- Calories: 180
- Protein: 6g
- Fat: 14g
- Carbohydrates: 8g
- Fiber: 4g
- Sugar: 3g
- Sodium: 0mg

COTTAGE CHEESE WITH PINEAPPLE CHUNKS

INGREDIENTS

- 1/2 cup cottage cheese
- 1/2 cup pineapple chunks

DIRECTIONS

1. Place cottage cheese in a bowl.
2. Top with pineapple chunks.

NUTRITIONAL INFORMATION

- Calories: 150
- Protein: 14g
- Fat: 2g
- Carbohydrates: 20g
- Fiber: 1g
- Sugar: 18g
- Sodium: 400mg (Sodium content may vary depending on the brand of cottage cheese)

HARD-BOILED EGGS

INGREDIENTS

- 2 eggs

DIRECTIONS

1. Put eggs in a pot and cover it with water.
2. Bring water to a boil, then reduce heat and simmer for 10–12 minutes.
3. Remove eggs from water and let cool before peeling.

NUTRITIONAL INFORMATION

- Calories: 140
- Protein: 12g
- Fat: 9g
- Carbohydrates: 1g
- Fiber: 0g
- Sugar: 0g
- Sodium: 124mg

Trail Mix with Nuts and Dried Fruit

INGREDIENTS

- 1/4 cup almonds
- 1/4 cup walnuts
- 1/4 cup dried cranberries
- 1/4 cup dried apricots, chopped

DIRECTIONS

1. Mix all the ingredients together in a bowl.

NUTRITIONAL INFORMATION

- Calories: 250
- Protein: 6g
- Fat: 17g
- Carbohydrates: 22g
- Fiber: 4g
- Sugar: 14g
- Sodium: 5mg

Roasted Chickpeas

INGREDIENTS

- 1 can (15 oz) chickpeas, drained and rinsed
- 1 tbsp olive oil
- 1 tsp paprika
- 1/2 tsp garlic powder
- 1/2 tsp cumin
- Salt-free seasoning blend, to taste

DIRECTIONS

1. Preheat oven to 400°F (200°C).
2. Pat chickpeas dry with paper towels and remove any loose skins.
3. In a bowl, toss chickpeas with olive oil and seasonings until evenly coated.
4. Spread the chickpeas in one layer on a baking sheet covered with parchment paper.
5. Roast for 20-25 minutes, shaking the pan halfway through, until chickpeas are crispy and golden brown.

NUTRITIONAL INFORMATION

- Calories: 200
- Protein: 7g
- Fat: 7g
- Carbohydrates: 28g
- Fiber: 8g
- Sugar: 6g
- Sodium: 15mg

Fruit Salad with Fresh Mint

INGREDIENTS

- 1 cup mixed fresh fruits (such as berries, melon, grapes, and kiwi), chopped
- Fresh mint leaves, for garnish

DIRECTIONS

1. Combine mixed fruits in a bowl.
2. Garnish with fresh mint leaves.

NUTRITIONAL INFORMATION

- Calories: 80
- Protein: 1g
- Fat: 0g
- Carbohydrates: 20g
- Fiber: 3g
- Sugar: 15g
- Sodium: 0mg

CHAPTER 7

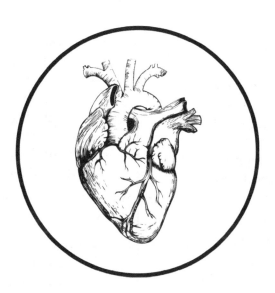

28 DAY MEAL PLAN

WEEK1

DAY1
- Breakfast: Oatmeal with Fresh Berries and Almonds..pg2
- Lunch: Grilled Chicken Salad with Avocado and Lime Dressing..pg13
- Snack: Apple Slices with Almond Butter..pg57
- Dinner: Grilled Lemon Herb Chicken with Roasted Vegetables..pg24

DAY2
- Breakfast: Greek Yogurt with Sliced Strawberries and Chia Seeds..pg3
- Lunch: Quinoa and Black Bean Stuffed Bell Peppers..pg14
- Snack: Carrot Sticks with Hummus..pg58
- Dinner: Baked Cod with Garlic and Herbs..pg25

DAY3
- Breakfast: Spinach and Mushroom Egg White Omelette..pg4
- Lunch: Baked Salmon with Asparagus and Lemon..pg15
- Snack: Greek Yogurt with Sliced Peaches..pg59
- Dinner: Spaghetti Squash with Tomato Basil Sauce..pg26

DAY4
- Breakfast: Avocado and Tomato on Whole Grain Toast..pg5
- Lunch: Turkey and Spinach Lettuce Wraps..pg16
- Snack: Rice Cakes with Avocado Mash..pg60
- Dinner: Turkey Meatloaf with Mashed Cauliflower..pg27

DAY5
- Breakfast: Fruit Smoothie with Kale and Flaxseed..pg6
- Lunch: Vegetable Stir-Fry with Tofu..pg17
- Snack: Celery Sticks with Peanut Butter..pg61
- Dinner: Stir-Fried Tofu with Broccoli and Bell Peppers..pg28

DAY6
- Breakfast: Quinoa Porridge with Apples and Cinnamon..pg7
- Lunch: Lentil Soup with Carrots and Celery..pg18
- Snack: Cottage Cheese with Pineapple Chunks..pg62
- Dinner: Roasted Vegetable Quinoa Bowl..pg29

DAY7
- Breakfast: Cottage Cheese with Pineapple and Walnuts..pg8
- Lunch: Chickpea and Tomato Salad with Olive Oil and Basil..pg19
- Snack: Hard-boiled Eggs..pg63
- Dinner: Lemon Garlic Shrimp with Steamed Asparagus..pg30

TO DO
- ○ _____
- ○ _____
- ○ _____
- ○ _____
- ○ _____

WEEK2

DAY8
- Breakfast: Banana Pancakes with Blueberries..pg9
- Lunch: Zucchini Noodles with Pesto and Cherry Tomatoes..pg20
- Snack: Trail Mix with Nuts and Dried Fruit..pg63
- Dinner: Oven-Roasted Chicken Thighs with Brussels Sprouts..pg31

DAY9
- Breakfast: Sweet Potato and Black Bean Breakfast Burrito..pg10
- Lunch: Chicken and Vegetable Skewers.pg21
- Snack: Roasted Chickpeas..pg64
- Dinner: Eggplant and Zucchini Ratatouille..pg32

DAY10
- Breakfast: Homemade Muesli with Almond Milk and Fresh Fruits..pg11
- Lunch: Eggplant and Tomato Bake with Fresh Herbs..pg22
- Snack: Fruit Salad with Fresh Mint..pg65
- Dinner: Lentil and Vegetable Curry..pg33

DAY11
- Breakfast: Oatmeal with Fresh Berries and Almonds..pg2
- Lunch: Grilled Chicken Salad with Avocado and Lime Dressing..pg13
- Snack: Apple Slices with Almond Butter..pg57
- Dinner: Grilled Lemon Herb Chicken with Roasted Vegetables..pg24

DAY12
- Breakfast: Greek Yogurt with Sliced Strawberries and Chia Seeds..pg3
- Lunch: Quinoa and Black Bean Stuffed Bell Peppers..pg14
- Snack: Carrot Sticks with Hummus..pg58
- Dinner: Baked Cod with Garlic and Herbs..pg25

DAY13
- Breakfast: Spinach and Mushroom Egg White Omelette..pg4
- Lunch: Baked Salmon with Asparagus and Lemon..pg15
- Snack: Greek Yogurt with Sliced Peaches..pg59
- Dinner: Spaghetti Squash with Tomato Basil Sauce..pg26

DAY14
- Breakfast: Avocado and Tomato on Whole Grain Toast..pg5
- Lunch: Turkey and Spinach Lettuce Wraps..pg16
- Snack: Rice Cakes with Avocado Mash..pg60
- Dinner: Turkey Meatloaf with Mashed Cauliflower..pg27

TO DO
- ○ _____
- ○ _____
- ○ _____
- ○ _____
- ○ _____

WEEK3

DAY15
- Breakfast: Fruit Smoothie with Kale and Flaxseed..pg6
- Lunch: Vegetable Stir-Fry with Tofu..pg17
- Snack: Celery Sticks with Peanut Butter..pg61
- Dinner: Stir-Fried Tofu with Broccoli and Bell Peppers..pg28

DAY16
- Breakfast: Quinoa Porridge with Apples and Cinnamon..pg7
- Lunch: Lentil Soup with Carrots and Celery..pg18
- Snack: Cottage Cheese with Pineapple Chunks..pg62
- Dinner: Roasted Vegetable Quinoa Bowl..pg29

DAY17
- Breakfast: Cottage Cheese with Pineapple and Walnuts..pg8
- Lunch: Chickpea and Tomato Salad with Olive Oil and Basil..pg19
- Snack: Hard-boiled Eggs..pg63
- Dinner: Lemon Garlic Shrimp with Steamed Asparagus..pg30

DAY18
- Breakfast: Banana Pancakes with Blueberries..pg9
- Lunch: Zucchini Noodles with Pesto and Cherry Tomatoes..pg20
- Snack: Trail Mix with Nuts and Dried Fruit..pg63
- Dinner: Oven-Roasted Chicken Thighs with Brussels Sprouts..pg31

DAY19
- Breakfast: Sweet Potato and Black Bean Breakfast Burrito..pg10
- Lunch: Chicken and Vegetable Skewers..pg21
- Snack: Roasted Chickpeas..pg64
- Dinner: Eggplant and Zucchini Ratatouille..pg32

DAY20
- Breakfast: Homemade Muesli with Almond Milk and Fresh Fruits..pg11
- Lunch: Eggplant and Tomato Bake with Fresh Herbs..pg22
- Snack: Fruit Salad with Fresh Mint..pg65
- Dinner: Lentil and Vegetable Curry..pg33

DAY21
- Breakfast: Oatmeal with Fresh Berries and Almonds..pg2
- Lunch: Grilled Chicken Salad with Avocado and Lime Dressing..pg13
- Snack: Apple Slices with Almond Butter..pg57
- Dinner: Grilled Lemon Herb Chicken with Roasted Vegetables..pg24

TO DO
- ○ _____
- ○ _____
- ○ _____
- ○ _____
- ○ _____

WEEK4

DAY22
- Breakfast: Greek Yogurt with Sliced Strawberries and Chia Seeds..pg3
- Lunch: Quinoa and Black Bean Stuffed Bell Peppers..pg14
- Snack: Carrot Sticks with Hummus..pg58
- Dinner: Baked Cod with Garlic and Herbs..pg25

DAY23
- Breakfast: Spinach and Mushroom Egg White Omelette..pg4
- Lunch: Baked Salmon with Asparagus and Lemon..pg15
- Snack: Greek Yogurt with Sliced Peaches..pg59
- Dinner: Spaghetti Squash with Tomato Basil Sauce..pg26

DAY24
- Breakfast: Avocado and Tomato on Whole Grain Toast..pg5
- Lunch: Turkey and Spinach Lettuce Wraps..pg16
- Snack: Rice Cakes with Avocado Mash..pg60
- Dinner: Turkey Meatloaf with Mashed Cauliflower..pg27

DAY25
- Breakfast: Fruit Smoothie with Kale and Flaxseed..pg6
- Lunch: Vegetable Stir-Fry with Tofu..pg17
- Snack: Celery Sticks with Peanut Butter..pg61
- Dinner: Stir-Fried Tofu with Broccoli and Bell Peppers..pg28

DAY26
- Breakfast: Quinoa Porridge with Apples and Cinnamon..pg7
- Lunch: Lentil Soup with Carrots and Celery..pg18
- Snack: Cottage Cheese with Pineapple Chunks..pg62
- Dinner: Roasted Vegetable Quinoa Bowl..29

DAY27
- Breakfast: Cottage Cheese with Pineapple and Walnuts..pg8
- Lunch: Chickpea and Tomato Salad with Olive Oil and Basil..pg19
- Snack: Hard-boiled Eggs..pg63
- Dinner: Lemon Garlic Shrimp with Steamed Asparagus..pg30

DAY28
- Breakfast: Banana Pancakes with Blueberries..pg9
- Lunch: Zucchini Noodles with Pesto and Cherry Tomatoes..pg20
- Snack: Trail Mix with Nuts and Dried Fruit..pg63
- Dinner: Oven-Roasted Chicken Thighs with Brussels Sprouts..pg31

TO DO
- ○ _____
- ○ _____
- ○ _____
- ○ _____
- ○ _____

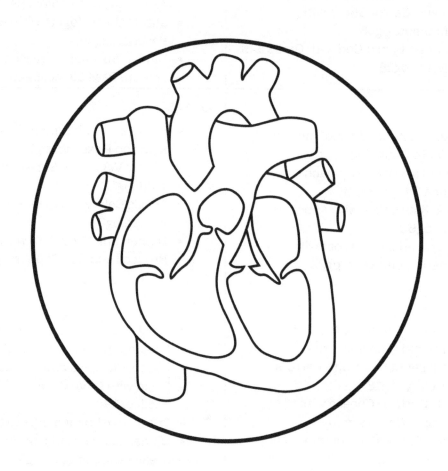